THE
WISHING BONE
CYCLE

THE
WISHING BONE
CYCLE

NARRATIVE POEMS FROM THE

Swampy Cree
Indians

GATHERED AND TRANSLATED BY

Howard A. Norman

PRE-FACE BY

JEROME ROTHENBERG

STONEHILL PUBLISHING COMPANY
NEW YORK

To Laurence and Estelle Norman

Thinking of Nibènegenesábe's (and others') repertoire of gestures and voices during his performances of tales, illuminates to me again the luxury of listening (partaking) in *telling* events, and, most especially of working *with* the one you translate from. I am grateful for the generosity and friendship of the Nibènegenesábe and other families who took me in so many times and for such long periods. I also wish to thank Dr. John McCafferty, whose knowledge of Canadian animals was vital; the Rothenberg family and T. Rinehart, who opened their homes to me during various periods of transiency and John Rains, for his immense help with the translations. During some of the final writing and translating work, I was supported by a fellowship from the Society of Fellows, University of Michigan.

Copyright © 1976 by Howard A. Norman. Published by the Stonehill Publishing Company, a division of Stonehill Communications, Inc., 38 East 57 Street, New York, N.Y. 10022.

ISBN: 0-88373-045-6 (hardcover)
ISBN: 0-88373-046-4 (softcover)
Library of Congress Catalog Card Number: 76-20335

Original woodcuts by William Threepersons; adapted for this edition by Howard A. Norman

Cover design by George Corsillo
Book design by Esther Mitgang and Heather White

First printing.

Printed in U.S.A.

The *Muska koo*, Swampy Cree, an Algonquian Indian people, are primarily hunters, trappers, and fishermen, whose communities (throughout history) have been located across the Canadian subarctic, from Hudson Bay's SW peripheral muskeg shields, through the central moist, coniferous forests, swamp and lake regions, and occasionally into the "Grove Belt" (poplar savannah) of southcentral Canada. The Swampy's dialect of Cree, in which the specific narratives (and songs) in this book were heard, is generally spoken in the north-central regions of the Province of Manitoba to the NE to Hudson Bay.

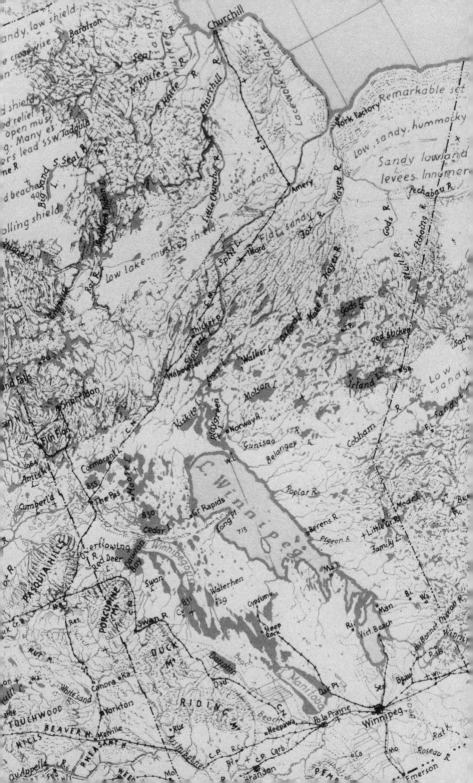

PRE-FACE

Our only measure of truth is ... our perception of truth. The undeniable tradition of metamorphosis teaches us that things do not remain always the same. They become other things by swift and unanalysable process. It was only when men began to mistrust the myths and tell nasty lies for a moral purpose that these matters became hopelessly confused. (Ezra Pound, 1918)

Take that as a start: Pound's version of what has come to be one of our chief poetic insights. A poetry of changes as a notion fundamental to our oldest memories as human beings. And that lovely condensation flashed to mind the first time I had a look at Howard Norman's versions from the Cree. Their beauty (gentle, crazy) was so much tied up with where they came from: not the contrivance of the kind of poetry sophisticates we're sometimes thought to be but of another breed of individuals who remain our masters. To get to where those others are, we've had to break the mind-set of our culture—doing that to re-invent what is still possible in theirs, adherence through tradition to what Cassirer called the "law of metamorphosis in thought & word."

Jacob Nibènegenesábe & Samuel Makidemewabe are traditional Cree story-tellers (oral poets, in brief), & Howard Norman is one who learns from them as well. The *telling* is for them & him & us an act of "going backward/looking forward," in which past & future intersect; in which traditional ways (as process) do not imprison but free the mind to new beginnings & speculations. This is the basis of the "oral" as a liberating possibility: an interplay that preserves the mind's capacity for transformation—as important in an ecological sense as that other preservation (of earth & living forms, etc.) that we now recognize not as nostalgia but a necessary tool for human survival. And that capacity is not a blind, collective process then or now—not by a long shot. The poets here represented are no automatons of culture but real people, individuals with names & voices & the power to invent & make things new. They are what Aristotle called the old Greek "tragic" poets (goat-song men): the makers (*poetes*) of the story (*mythos*), i.e., the poets of the myth. The implications of *all* of that is what this book is secretly about.

So if you read on, you'll see that the culture doesn't so much provide the stories (only the long tale about the walking trickster is so handed down, & even there the stress on the performance makes it different every time) as the capacity to make & tell them. The Wishing Bone Cycle (Nibènegenesábe's masterwork) is the best instance of the way it goes.

The process? Well, start with a single, not too implausible, event, & turn it. See what can go wrong. A kind of test of circumstance. Thus: wish or think up a hammock for a tired man. But the hammock is a whole valley—initial complication—and there's snow in it. That's trouble. And around the valley & the sleeping man are wolves. So make a further complication for the fun, the play of it, & give the man a pair of antlers. Let him start farting like a moose (why not?) until the wolves get curious. But add a further complication still: when they get there they can't see the man. So have him sneeze, & so on.

The meaning (no "moral" but "meaning") is tied to the quick changes. And the changes are everywhere & are a testimony to a view of life which finds us all in motion for as long as we can think & speak of it. The trickster of the final story is the religious embodiment of that process—as the "wishing bone" is Nibènegenesábe's personal one. He is not like the god we know, but one who changes (himself & others) & often does it badly. (Or in that sense: he is *really* like the god we know; only he doesn't have to keep up a front.) The moral is happily deferred, but the energies are undeniable & very human.

Those energies of course are what informs the one who tells about them & the ones who learn by listening. In their transmission—which is what our lives are all about in art & poetry—the messages continue & are changed. They also change the tellers, in this instance Howard Norman. For he has learned, as he would have had to, not merely to translate spoken words into written, but at the insistence of his teacher's (story-tellers he has known from childhood) to tell the tale himself. I think of him as I first got to know him: telling the stories of the wishing bone or sitting at a table with a stack of wishing bones provided by old friends in gratitude. *I wished the wishing bones to be a book of words, & here it is. And now I wish the words to speak, & when they do I wish they all speak with your voice. I wish you all to tell their story & your own.*

JEROME ROTHENBERG

January 1976

xi

THE WISHING BONE CYCLE:
"Trickster" Narratives

*T*HE *Wishing Bone poems constitute a "trickster
cycle," one of the oldest traditional genres of Cree
oral literature. The inventor and initiator of these particular
poems was Jacob Nibènegenesábe, who lived for ninety-four
years northeast of Lake Winnipeg, Canada. Nibènegenesábe
was considered an excellent* teller *(àchimoo) of the more
traditional narratives, as represented by the last tale in this
book. Although I never asked his reasons for originating
the Wishing Bone poems, I would say he obviously enjoyed
the wide latitude of invention the concept of a "wishing
bone" afforded him. One might also point to statements of
his, such as: "I was curious to tell things past the old oth-
ers" (meaning: things not discussed in older tales). And,
further: "Someone comes to ask me 'How did this or that
happen?' At first I might not know the answer. But later
these stories let me remember." He often made comments
on his* tellings *of the Wishing Bone poems, never solely to
assign them some historical validity but to acknowledge
continually the contagious, fertile procedure of "thinking
things up."*

*The following explanation is a paraphrase, combined
from several conversations with Nibènegenesábe, concern-
ing the discovery of the "wishing bone" itself:*

*One spring, near Lake Winnipeg, a single snow goose
appeared high in the air. It glided down on a smaller
lake and swam to shore. Nearby and quietly, a lynx
crouched as the wind shifted the goose's scent into his
nose. For a brief moment the goose lifted its head,
listening. But before it could rise again safely, the lynx*

3

had it in his teeth. *The lynx feasted down to bones and feathers. Then, just as he began to crack a bone for marrow, a man called out and the lynx was quick into the trees. Only artifacts of the goose remained, but among them the man found a bone said to protect the heart—a "wishing bone." He examined it slowly. Later, he found that the bone was a tool of metamorphosis which allowed him to become a "trickster" capable of wishing things into existence, and himself into various situations. These stories are about him.*

The Swampy Cree have a conceptual term which I've heard used to describe the thinking of a porcupine as he backs into a rock crevice: Usá puyew usu wapiw (*"He goes backward, looks forward"*). *The porcupine consciously goes backward in order to speculate safely on the future, allowing him to look out at his enemy or just the new day. To the Cree, it's an instructive act of self-preservation. Nibènegenesábe's opening formula for the Wishing Bone poems (and other tales) consisted of an invitation to listen* (Nutoka moo), *followed by the phrase: "I go backward, look forward, as the porcupine does." The idea is that each time these stories about the past are told they will be learned for the future.*

I try to make wishes right
but sometimes it doesn't work.
Once, I wished a tree upside down
and its branches
were where the roots should have been!
The squirrels had to ask the moles
"How do we get down there
to get home?"
One time it happened that way.
Then there was the time, I remember now,
I wished a man upside down
and his feet were where his hands
should have been!
In the morning his shoes
had to ask the birds
"How do we fly up there
to get home?"
One time it happened that way.

This is for turtles, that's why
I'm telling it close to water.
Next time I might stick my head right in!
I say this
"Turtle, you bite me again
it's trouble!
I see you laughing those bubbles.
They come up and I break them
and laughing comes out.
Yesterday I was with my toes
in the river
and drinking some sun
from the top of the water.
Otter was there too with his toes.
But you got my toes!
Did you make a deal with Otter?"

One time I wished myself
into a moose deer.
I was lying down and sleeping
with my own shadow
and then you came along
saying the sun was in your mouth,
saying you were thirsty!
I wished you to where you drank tears.
It was a lake
everyone cried into,
full of people's tears.
At night
some of the tears left
to look for sad faces
to fall down.
Then the whole lake cried.
Some said it was the loons.

One time I wished myself in love.
I was the little squirrel
with dark stripes.
I climbed shaky limbs for fruit for her.
I even swam with the moon on the water
to reach her.
That was a time little troubled me.
I worked all day to gather food
and watched her sleep all night.
It is not the same way now
but my heart still sings
when I hear her
over the leaves.

There was a storm once.
That's when I wished myself
into a turtle.
But I meant on land!
The one that carries a hard tent
on his back.
I didn't want to be floating!
I wanted to pull everything inside
and dry.
Here comes the waves
shaking me,
and I'm getting sick in the insides.
I wanted to be the turtle
eating buds and flowers and berries.
I've got to wish things exactly!
That's the way it is
from now on.

One time I saw
a tree with no animals in it.
I started walking around it.
That's when each of my eyes
saw a different animal,
a bird and a porcupine.
So I wished them up in that tree.
But only one animal got up there.
He was a porcupine and bird in the same body!
How did that happen?
He flew up and got stuck in the clouds
with his quills.
Then he came down into some bush thorns
and lost some feathers.
The only place he could live
was in that tree.
He made friends with the wind there.
When the wind came
to shake the tree
the wind cleaned his quills.
When the wind came
looking for someone to fly with
under the clouds
the animal went.

I'll tell you
how that salamander got legs.
It was a worm once.
I'll say that first.
A fat worm.
One day it came up to see
if the ground
still had sun on it.
That's when a bird came after it.
The worm crawled slow
looking for a hole.
But its tail and head found a hole
at the same time!
It was going two ways
into the ground
and stretching.
Here comes the bird!
So I wished the worm some legs
and it ran under a log.
Later, it lived in a wet stump.
Then I wished salamanders all over
sleeping under leaves
with their eyes and tails and legs.
But the worm
is still inside them somewhere.

One night I was wishing things all over.
Then, I thought there were too many stars
in the sky
and not enough light down under,
in the earth.
That's when I wished a star down
for that mole
to carry on his nose.
He took it down under.
He walked around with it under there
and tried it out.
Now he comes up sometimes
to let his star talk to the other stars
in the sky.
It's dark down there
but his nose sees where he's going.

A snake lost his eyes once.
Don't blame this one on me!
It was the snowy owl.
He was playing the moon.
That owl closed his eyes
and sat in a fog tree
with his white face.
The snake looked up through the fog
and saw that round face
and said, "Moon, show me a meal!"
Then that moon came down and took his eyes.

One time I was tired of being young.
So, I wished myself into an old man.
But I was dying!
The children gathered around
saying
"Do not die.
Let's go out and have a day.
Look! the moon is forgiving us
with another sun."
But I was sweating, and said
"It is time.
That log has hollowed itself out
and waits for me.
My old spirit already has its shoes on."
Then I crawled into the log
with the moon just beginning
to forgive me.

Sure I saw the water monster!
Why do you think I got back here so fast?
Yes, that was me
sitting in a tree by the lake
wishing myself into a walking stick
and making cracking-leaves sounds
and making wishes on myself.
That's when I saw him!
I couldn't think straight so thought crooked,
which is how I got to be
a snake
come winding out
and safe at home.
All because I saw him.

Once when I was walking
I saw an owl-beak
with no owl-face around it!
It was sitting
in a tree
and singing.
This wasn't my trick!
I'd never leave my mouth
up in a tree
just to come down to the ground
to hear it sing.
Then the beak flew down onto a mouse.
I sure wasn't that hungry.
It wasn't me.
Then the beak
flew up to a hole nest in a tree
with two little owl-beaks in it.
They were hungry
and ate up the mouse.
This really happened!
It wasn't my doing, heh heh.

I'll tell you what it's like
being the biggest fish
in the lake.
I know this, since I wished myself
to be a sturgeon.
The smaller fish call me
with their voices,
and the water birds too.
"Your big mouth,
use it to eat our enemies!"
That's what they say.
But then I get hungry for them!

One day I wished myself
among frogs
and have been living with them
trying to get their medicine.
A day a while ago
I left the swamp and returned home.
But all my wife wanted
was my legs!
She said
"YOU LOOK LIKE A FROG NOW!"
Now I'm back
trying to get the medicine.
It's been half my life now.
Do you think they're tricking me?

Once there was a duck who lightened up the swamp.
I just happened to be there.
"Ho! lantern on the water!"
some men called.

But the duck said nothing.
It sat deep
in the swamp
and glowed.

"It's where the sun goes at night!"
one man called, "inside that duck!"
Then he called
"We know you've swallowed the sun, duck.
Let it go. It's near morning!"

But the duck said nothing.
It lightened up the swamp.

Then the men tried to capture the duck.
They grew very quiet, and got close.
Then they leaped toward the duck,
but all they caught
was mud in their mouths.

"Look, over there!" one man called.
Then they saw the duck sitting far away
on the water.
It was lighting up the swamp again!

I just happened to be there.
But in the morning we were both gone.

There was an old woman I wished up.
She was the wife
of an old pond.
You could watch her swim in her husband
if you were
in the hiding bushes.
She spoke to him by the way she swam
gently.
One time in their lives there was no rain
and the sun began making the pond smaller.
Soon the sun took the whole pond!
For many nights the old woman slept
near the hole where her husband once lived.
Then, one night, a storm came
but in the morning there still was no water
in her husband's old house.
So she set out on a journey to find her husband
and followed the puddles on the ground
which were the storm's footprints.
She followed them for many miles.
Finally she came upon her husband
sitting in a hole. But he was in the wrong hole!
So the old woman brought her husband home
little by little in her hands.
You could have seen him come home
if you were
in the hiding bushes.

One day I wished
that the squirrels all had their tails
pointing north.
I made them point north just by wishing it!
It looked as if a wind was blowing north
and trying to take those squirrel tails
with it.
I walked down a path
and saw squirrels in trees and on the ground.
All with their tails pointing north.

"It's so strange
you would do this to us,"
one squirrel said.

I said, "I got lost once, and couldn't find north.
If that ever happens again, I'll just follow
your tails."

Then the squirrels called someone
for help. It was a skunk!
I wasn't too happy about this.

I was standing just north
of that skunk, close to him.
He said, "Let their tails go!
I'll show you which way
north is."

Then he pointed his tail north.
At me!

I wished the squirrel tails back
their old way.

The skunk still had his tail
pointed at me.
I tried to get away, but it was too late.

Awgh! I ran south
shouting, "He sprayed me!"

For days everyone knew
in their noses
which way south was,
because of me.

I went around the village
bragging that I had the best ears,
that I could hear things
in the distance before anyone.
And I was right! Until the lynx came along.
He walked in and said, "I have better ears."
So, we had a contest. Both of us
sat in the middle of the village,
listening.
I wished mud into the lynx's ears
but he cleaned it out.
Then I saw his ears lean!
He was hearing something.
He kept hearing it
and leaning his ears.
I wished whitefish oil, mud, and moss
into his ears
but it was too late.
Finally, he said, "A wolf has just given up
hunting
at the beaver pond."
Everyone was puzzled.

"I didn't hear anything," I said.

"I heard the whole thing
happen," he said,
as he was cleaning his ears again.

Then, one man left for the beaver pond.
He came back and said, "It's true!
There are wolf tracks all around,
and so much tail-slapping went on
by those beavers to warn each other,
that there are big waves in the pond!"

23

"I heard it all along,"
the lynx said.

I got angry. I said, "The wolf told him
where he was going to hunt ahead of time . . . no,
I mean the beavers knew . . . no, I mean that mud
I wished into his ears somehow helped him . . .
what I mean is, there should be another contest
to give me a fair chance!"

But it was too late. They all
had put mud in their ears
not to listen to me.

One time I wished up
a footprint tree.
It had the footprints of many animals
for leaves.
Footprints left behind
in mud and snow
were all hanging on that tree!
I wished all kinds of weather
into that tree, too.
It stayed cold
around the snow footprints
and warmer
around the mud footprints.
I wanted them to stay just as they were
when they were left behind.
That is how it was in the tree.
When a bear walked by
some old bear tracks
would leap off the tree
and come sniffing up to its feet!
They would be looking
for a home.
If the bear was the same one
who left them behind
long ago
they would leap back on
the bear's feet
and go back to living there.
Until the bear walked in snow
or mud again.
Those leaves leaped down!
Bear footprints
made a loud sound
when they hit the ground
and often

bird footprints flew away in the wind
trying to catch up with birds!
Bird-footprint leaves could be seen floating
in the air!
I tell you I was happy after wishing that tree up!
Except, later, I had leaves
from the mud and snow I'd walked in
sniffing around my feet too.

There was a man who was very tired.
So, I wished him up
a hammock.
It was a whole valley!
With snow!
This hammock was held up by pine trees
at both ends
and I wished him down there
sleeping in it.
He slept in the center of this hammock
even though wolves
were gathering on its rim.
He went on sleeping!
So, for fun, I wished some antlers
on that man
and made him fart out like a moose!
The wolves were puzzled
but interested.
The man went on sleeping.
Then, the wolves began to run down
into the valley
to investigate this.
That's when I wished a tremendous snow storm up!
The wolves could not see the man
or each other. And, to make things more interesting,
I wished the man sneezing in echoes!
Echoes were flying all over the valley.
Sneeze echoes!
The wolves began blaming each other
for making too much noise
on this hunt.
"Stop sneezing!" one wolf called
to another wolf.
"No, you stop sneezing!" the wolf said back.
I can't begin to tell you

how I was laughing at this
the whole time!
The man went on sleeping and causing trouble.
The wolves finally gave up
and went back up the hill.
The crows who watched this whole thing too
never did let those wolves forget it.
You could always hear those crows
teasing.
And that man,
he just went on sleeping.
Until I wished him awake.
I don't think he ever knew what went on.

One time I wanted two moons
in the sky.
But I needed someone to look up and see
those two moons
because I wanted to hear him
try and convince the others in the village
of what he saw.
I knew it would be funny.
So, I did it.
I wished another moon up!
There it was, across the sky from the old moon.
Along came a man.
Of course I wished him down that open path.
He looked up in the sky.
He had to see that other moon!
One moon for each of his eyes!
He stood looking
up in the sky
a long time.
Then he suspected me, I think.
He looked into the trees
where he thought I might be.
But he could not see me
since I was disguised as the whole night itself!
Sometimes
I wish myself into looking like the whole day,
but this time
I was dressed like the whole night.
Then he said,
"There is something strange
in the sky tonight."
He said it out loud.
I heard it clearly.
Then he hurried home
and I followed him.

He told the others, "You will not believe this,
but there are ONLY two moons
in the sky tonight."
He had a funny look on his face.
Then, all the others began looking into the woods.
Looking for me, no doubt!
"Only two moons, ha! Who can believe you?
We won't fall for that!" they all said to him.
They were trying to send the trick back at me!
This was clear to me!
So, I quickly wished a third moon up there
in the sky.
They looked up and saw three moons.
They had to see them!
Then one man
said out loud, "Ah, there, look up!
up there!
There is only one moon!
Well, let's go sleep on this
and in the morning
we will try and figure it out."
They all agreed, and went in their houses
to sleep.
I was left standing there
with three moons shining on me.
There were three . . . I was sure of it.

There were two caribou deer
fighting with their antlers.
I was out walking
and heard them crashing
into each other.
"What are you fighting over?" I asked,
"I'm interested."
Both of them stopped
and turned their antlers toward me!
I figured out which tree to climb
quickly.
From up there I wished their antlers
locked together!
"I think we're stuck," one said.
Dust was still flying up
all around
from their fighting
and going into their mouths.
"Well, I'm thirsty
and I'm going to the lily pad lake
to drink.
It's my favorite place."
Then he began to walk
toward the lily pad lake.
"Wait!" the other caribou said,
"I want to go to the lake
pine cones
are often floating on!
The water there is sweet and good."
Then that caribou
began heading toward the pine cone lake.
They were both trying
to drag each other
a different way!
They were getting nowhere.

31

They made a nice dust-swirl storm again though.
"This dust
is getting us more thirsty!" one said.
It was time
for me to help out,
but not completely.
So, I wished both of their favorite lakes
close to them.
Those caribou were on a small piece of dry land
between two lakes!
Their thirst was growing more, too,
because they were so close to the water now.
Then I appeared in front of them.
"All right, I'll tell you
what we were fighting about
if you'll wish us
out of this mess!" one caribou said to me.
I agreed to it.
He said,
"We were fighting about which lake
was best to drink from. That's what."
I didn't believe him
but enjoyed
his quick thinking.
"Sometimes it's the lake
you are closest to,"
I said.
Then I wished their antlers apart.
As I left, they both were drinking.

Once I wished up a coat
wearing a man inside.
The man was sleeping
and when he woke
the coat was on him!
This was in summer, so many asked him
"Why do you have that coat on?"
"It has me in it!"
he would answer.
He tried to take it off
but I wished his memory shivering with cold
so it wouldn't want to remember
how to take a coat off.
That way it would stay warm.
I congratulated myself on thinking of that.
Then his friends came,
put coats on,
and slowly showed him how they took coats off.
Even that didn't work.
Things were getting interesting.
Then his friends
tried to confuse the coat
into thinking it was a man.
"Good morning," they said to it,
"Did you get
your share of fish?"
and other things too.
Some even invited the coat to gossip.
It got to be late summer
and someone said to the coat
"It is getting colder.
You better go out
and find a coat to wear."

The coat agreed!

Ha! I was too busy laughing
to stop that dumb coat
from leaving the man it wore
inside.
I didn't care.
I went following the coat.
Things were getting interesting.

There was a man
having much trouble hunting.
Of course I was the cause of his trouble.
If he came upon a deer
I'd make him very clumsy
and he would stumble
or step on a twig.
The deer ran off!
If he came upon a family of pheasants
I'd wish a lynx
leaping right in the middle of them
and they would scatter and fly!
The man grew very confused.
Then, I switched things around.
I made things very easy for him.
If he went out
to hunt deer
I would make the shape of a deer
out of the dust.
Then those dust deer led him to the real deer!
Just up ahead!
See how that worked?
I made pheasants out of leaves
which swirled toward
the real pheasants!
And one time he came upon a trout made of wood
hovering above a lake
he never knew trout lived in!
But he fished there and caught many!
The man knew
it was me doing this for him.
He said, "You are just helping me now
so I will trust you
and you can trick me good later on!"
But I hadn't thought of that.
Until then.

35

One day I came upon a flock of crows.
They were sitting on snow
and making crow noises.
I could see them clearly on white snow
This gave me an idea.
I wished those crows white,
except for their beaks.
I left the beaks black in color.
Then I called
to them,
"Crows, you are white!"
They looked at each other
and saw it was true.
It so happened
a coyote was out looking
for something to eat.
The coyote was coming their way.
The crows saw him
and said, "Let's fly up!"
But that
was too easy.
I wished their wings frozen.
They couldn't fly.
So, they stuck their black beaks
into the snow
so only their white bodies were sticking up.
The whole flock
did this!
And the coyote walked right past them!
Sure, he stopped
and sniffed the air.
He knew those crows were around somewhere
but he couldn't see them
against the snow.
I bet the crows really thought they were safe then.

But no,
that was too easy.
I wished all the snow around them
melted
and there were those crows
stuck in the ground
by their beaks!
They were still white so were seen clearly now!
The coyote turned around quickly.
He started for them.
But that was too easy
since those crows
were stuck in the ground.
So, I wished a steep hill in front
of the coyote.
The steepest hill around.
Then I called to him,
"You are very old, coyote,
and this might be
the hill you die on
trying to get to those crows!"
He had a decision to make then.
It wasn't easy.
I watched.
The crows waited, stuck by their beaks.
Everyone's heart beat fast.
Finally, the coyote said,
"I'm not hungry enough
to die on this hill,"
and he trotted off.
Then I wished the crows free too.
After all that.

One time
all the noises met.
All the noises in the world
met in one place
and I was there
because they met in my house.
My wife said, "Who sent them?"
I said, "Fox or Rabbit,
yes one of those two.
They're both out for tricking me back today.
Both of them
are mad at me.
Rabbit is mad because I pulled
his brother's ear
and held him up that way.
Then I ate him.
And Fox is mad because he wanted
to do those things first."

"Yes, then it had to be one of them,"
my wife said.

So, all the noises
were there.
These things happen.
Falling-tree noise was there.
Falling-rock noise was there.
Otter-mud-sliding noise was there.
All those noises, and more,
in my house.

"How long do you expect to stay?"
my wife asked them. "We need some sleep!"

They all answered at once!

That's why now my wife and I
sometimes can't hear well.
I should have wished them all away
first thing.

One night
a bear was standing in a field.
There was a full moon out.
Suddenly, the hair on top of the bear's head
flew up toward the moon!
I turned away quickly
and pretended to be taking a thorn
out of my foot.
The bear
saw his hair floating in moonlight.
He climbed a tree
and as he got close to his hair
more flew off toward the moon!
I was still taking the thorn out of my foot.
"You took my hair,"
the bear called down to me.
"No, the moon
took it," I answered.
The bear
climbed higher in the tree.
"I wouldn't advise that!" I called,
"That moon
wants you on it!"
The bear climbed higher.
I couldn't help myself.
I wished him floating in the moonlight!
First, I made him rise in the air.
Then I let him down lower.
I did this many times.
I kept working at the thorn in my foot
the whole time.
"O.K. moon, either take me
or let me down!" the bear shouted.
I wished him down.

Then he came running toward me!
He knew it was me tricking him!
I ran. You should have seen me run!
"You sure run quickly
with a thorn
in your foot!" the bear called
after me.

This happened in autumn.
I was looking for something to do
Then I saw a man go out
to gather sticks
for his fire.
Well, he found a good stick
and leaned down
to pick it up.
It flew up and turned into a bird!
When he turned back
to the pile of sticks
he had gathered
they all were flying!
In a circle they flew, high in the air!
Some landed in trees.
Some began singing.
One built a nest
made out of
a bunch of the others!
I was there
and happy my wishing was going so well
This was in autumn, I say again.
Some flocks were leaving
south.
You should have seen the look
on his face
when he saw those sticks flying south too!
Right behind some geese!
Ha!
One more good wish to do next year
on someone else.

"I see you bird bones!
You better get up and back together!
Where are the feathers?
It's cold and my teeth are rattling
the rest of me.
The ice trees are coming
and the weasel has his snow
all over him already!"
I said this at the beginning of winter.
I found those other bones lying there
and leaped in with them.
Then we went looking for the feathers.
I had my sack of old wishes with me.
Then, we found the feathers.
They were on a little tree
that had no leaves, and trying
to make it fly!
Ha! They thought those twigs were bones!
Then all the feathers leaped on us
and we flew south. This is what happened.
This is how I went to make wishes somewhere else.
I brought my sack of old wishes with me.

BORN TYING KNOTS:
Personal Name Origins

To say the name is to begin the story.

*A*FFILIATIONS *with animals are the most common sources of Swampy Cree personal names (i.e., those not designated under the auspices of the church). The names are acquired several ways. A boy called "Loud Lynx," for example, may have inherited the name from a grandfather who said it still had useful powers. Or his parents may have requested a shaman to interpret his next dream or vision into a name.[1] In this case, the shaman consents, and in the dream or vision a loud lynx indeed appears. The shaman would then have carried out his responsibility in naming the child accordingly. In either case, however, the boy lives under the protection and guidance of the lynx.[2]*

The name "Born Tying Knots" was given (without the aid of a shaman) because of an incident at birth in which the umbilical cord was knotted around the baby's toes. Subsequently,

> *. . . he heard his birth*
> *story.*
> *It caused him to begin tying knots again.*
> *He tied things up near his home,*
> *TIGHT, as if everything might float away*
> *in a river.*

In this way one is led to speculate upon the ways names

---

[1] *The dream, or vision, might not include an animal at all. The name "Turned Over Twice," for instance, came out of a shaman's vision of a boy sleeping near a cliff. The boy (in the vision) turned over once, nearing the cliff-edge, then turned back over safely. I never found out if the vision (and, consequently, the name) was in fact oracular.*

[2] *I use the lynx in the general sense of an animal namesake. Affiliations with specific animals are complex or simple, depending on the position and power of that animal as a totem figure.*

affect subsequent behavior (or to consider how much any name-origin is simply the teller's embellishment).

The following account of an entirely different but coincidental kind of meaning event was told in August, 1973, by Yakwama yetum ("He Is Cautious"):

I'd found a good name to fill up with someone. I'll tell you about it. I was standing on a high place, much to the north. I was travelling there, in that northern land. I saw a herd of caribou. They were feeding. There were many but I picked one out and watched him. Soon, the reason I picked him out became clear me. He began ajerking his head up and down fast. He did this many times. Also, he tried to trip one front leg with the other (as if) trying to trip himself! The whole herd was moving slowly. They were walking. But this was not enough moving for him. No, he had to be restless in other ways. I watched him more. Then I went back home. I told some new parents: I have a good, strong name. It is "Restless Caribou." They took the name for their son. This was after I told them the story. That's what happened.

On the other hand, if any unnamed boy (say, among a group of playing children)[3] was observed to be especially restless, it would be feasible to name him "Restless Caribou." In this way he "earns" (kuskëtumowab) the name for himself.

All of the name-origins translated in this chapter are earned names derived from various childhood episodes, affinities, special talents, even obsessions. Samuel Makideme-

---

[3] *I purposely use* group *as a correlate to* herd *because personal namings (and tales, songs, etc.) are often acutely attentive to animal behavior.*

wabe, in his capacity as one of the tribal historians, was invited to many naming ceremonies, at which the circumstances initiating each name were told to him. Or, as he said: "Names were brought to me from all over." You will notice that Makidemewabe spoke of all these naming incidents as if they occurred in his presence, which to him was less a matter of fact than a way of becoming intimate with the story. "I brought these stories home," he said, "and tell them here."[4]

Makidemewabe said: "To say the name is to begin the story." Over the years, I heard many personal names, then brought them to Makidemewabe. For me, then, to bring the name was to hear the story. This worked several ways. Often he would have his facts about a particular name right at hand. Other times, he would ask for time to "recall" the name's story. Though it was never requested, I told each story back to him many times in Cree before translating.

Finally, words Makidemewabe spoke loudly in his tellings are represented in my translations by capital letters; those he spoke softly, by italics.

[4] Makidemewabe lived mainly in two communities: one near Walker Lake, the other north of the Hayes River in Manitoba.

TREE OLD WOMAN

She stood close to a tree and wrinkled
her face, TIGHT,
and this was her tree-bark face.
It felt like bark, too, when you ran fingers
over it.

Tree old woman,
even when she was young.

Then her face would smooth out
into a young girl again. Once, after doing
her tree-bark face, she said,
"I *was* a tree and I saw a woodpecker
who wanted my head! That's why
I smoothed out my face so quickly!"

We looked up in the trees for that woodpecker,
but it wasn't there. So, our eyes
turned back to her. She was gone too!
We found her in a lake. She was holding on
to some shore reeds
with her legs floating out behind.
She looked up at us WITH THE WRINKLED FACE
OF A FROG! We were certain of it!
Then she smoothed her face out,
saying, "The largest turtle in the world
was swimming for me, thinking I was a frog!
That's why I smoothed my face out
so quickly!"

We didn't even look
for that turtle.

This time we kept our eyes on her
as she went to sit
by an old man, the oldest
in the village.
She sat down next to him.

Their two faces were close together,
and hers began
to wrinkle up again.

SAT IN THE CENTER

This boy went out in a snow blizzard
to catch fish. He went out on the swamp ice
and brought his chisel with him
to dig a hole through it.
He went singing.
In summer we could hear that swamp
sing all its birds and frogs together,
BUT THIS WAS IN WINTER.
He was the only one singing.

We heard him dig the hole
in the distance, but could not see this.
It was a chewing sound
his work made. After a while we got worried
he fell in,
or that the snow snakes
curled him away.

Worried we would never again
see him bob up among the wood duck
decoys, LAUGHING!
In summer.

He stayed out on the ice
until night. Then we saw his torch-stick fire
moving toward us,
and he came back home to put the fish he caught
on the fire.
Our worrying did not stop there.
He sat with us and watched the fish
thaw and cook.

He sat with us
in the center, shivering.
Then, we heard his laughter thaw out!
That's when our worrying stopped.

RAIN STRAIGHT DOWN

For a long time we thought this boy
loved only things that fell
straight down. He didn't seem to care
about anything else.

We were afraid he could only HEAR
things that fell straight down!

We watched him stand outside
in rain. Later, it was said
he put a tiny pond of rain water
in his wife's ear
while she slept. And leaned over
to listen to it.

I remember he was happiest talking
about all the kinds of rain.

The kind that comes off herons' wings
when they fly up from a lake. I know
he wanted some of that heron rain
for his wife's ear too!

He walked out in spring to watch
the young girls rub wild onion under their eyes
until tears came out.
He knew a name for that rain too.

Sad onion rain.

That rain fell straight down
too, off their faces,
and he saw it.

WHOSE WEAVING MELTED

Even when the coldest day of that winter
waited for her toes and face
she carried two quill needles
outside
and tried to weave a blanket
out of snow. She tried it that way.
Soon she found she had to use her hands
to *pack* the snow together, though,
and packed it on her sled
in the shape of a blanket.

She could not have tried harder
to weave snow.

But when she pulled *that* blanket home
on her sled, and brought it inside
to sleep under, it MELTED
and ended up in soup broth!

Still, she did not want to use
the same things everyone else used
for weaving.

So, later, she gathered some
of her family and friends outside
and tried to weave together
the cold breath steam
you could SEE
coming out of their noses and mouths
into the air.

She went from one person to the other
QUICKLY, trying to weave together

the breaths you could see. It was taking
a long time, and no
one could tell
how it was going! Each piece of weaving-breath
melted too, into the air, and stopped
coming out altogether
once everyone took his nose and mouth
inside.

BORN TYING KNOTS

When he came out, into the world,
the umbilical cord
was around his toes.
This didn't trouble us,
that he was tying knots *that* early.
We untied it.

Later, he heard his birth
story.
It caused him to begin tying knots again.
He tied things up near his home,
TIGHT, as if everything might float away
in a river.

This river came from
a dream he had.

House things were tied up
at night. Shirts, other clothes too,
and a kettle. All those things
were tied to his feet
so they wouldn't float away
in the river he dreamed.
You could walk in
and see this.

Maybe the dream stopped
because it was no longer comfortable
to sleep with shirts tied to him.
Or a kettle.

After the dream stopped,
he quit tying things,

EXCEPT for the one night he tied up
a small fire.
Tied up a small-stick fire!
The fire got loose its own way.

WALKED TOWARD THE LYNX

He knew a lynx has two voices.
There is one that is a growl
and can teach a baby pheasant to fly QUICKLY,
and frightens us too, sometimes.
And one other voice. It is when a lynx
scratches its claws on bark.

This boy would hear that scratching
and walk toward it.

If he *was* a lynx-ear
he could have heard it close up!
Or a whisker.

Which is what he wanted,
I think.

I saw him climb trees where he'd seen
a lynx, and find the place
where the scratch marks were left.
Then he would rub his fingers over them.
One finger at a time, gently,
or all of them at once.
His fingers heard the lynx talk again
that way.

TURTLE WAIT

He always watched
turtles. One lived around here,
the one who caused his name.

At an early age he waited for turtles
to come up on their logs.
Everyone knew this
about him. He'd wait. Wait. And one turtle
would be the last out of the water.
He had moss, mud, sometimes sticks
on his back
and he was a slow one.

Other turtle watchers gave up. But he would
wait until *that* turtle came out
to tell *him* things
and no one else.

So, in that way the turtle
caused his name.
The last one to wait for.

Up on his rock or log.

MANY TALKS

This girl did not give up baskets easily.
She sewed many, and also traded for them
in this village
and all over, in other villages.
The baskets sat in rows on the ground,
each filled with talk. You see,
she put something important to her
in each basket. Something from her life.
Then you could pick one out
for her to talk about,
just by lifting the cover!

That way you let the talk out.

This is how she had many mouths
sitting in rows on the ground.

The time I picked one it had
a catfish skull in it!
She told about catching this fish
who was GRINNING under some rocks
when she caught it.
It was the first fish she ever caught.

She grinned all through
the telling.

WHO ONCE LIVED ALONE

One summer this boy chose to live
by himself. It was never a secret, no, he just
said, "I'm going to live
by the next lake, to the north."
We could tell he had thought about it
a long time. He built a dwelling there.
It had rain fall on it, and had sun fall on it.
And the foxes didn't try to move in,
so, then for certain, it was his home.
He lived there all summer. We seldom heard him,
or knew where he was, except some nights
we knew he was out on the lake
because the loons were quiet.

There also were nights we wondered
how well he was eating, and that's when
we walked to where he lived.

Walked out at night to see
the bending pole. It was a pole
he had stuck in the ground.

This came about because he fished with long
stick poles, and he had stuck one of them
in the ground near his dwelling. After each day's fishing
he bent *that* pole to let us know his luck.
When it was bent low by rocks tied to its string,
we knew
he was catching fish.

When the pole was straight up,
we left fish
for him.

FOLLOWED THE HERON SHADE

She knew two herons flew over
each morning, and sent their shadows
along the ground below them.

Those birds were going
to meet the cool mud
with their feet, in a far place
I still know about. But I don't walk there anymore
because my ankles are too old.

She would wake early and run
after their shadows, trying to keep
in their shade!

This was moving heron shade
she chased
along the ground.

Each time she had to stop at the edge
of a lake, and watch those shadows
float out
and become rafts shaped like herons
on the water.

That's what happened.
Finally, we saw how those herons
were giving us her name.

MANY VOICES

We were out gathering full ripe
berries.
The black ones with spitting seeds
in them. We were gathering those berries.
That's when she made a voice.
Her first one of the day!
It was not her own human voice, BUT IT CAME
OUT OF HER! It was fox-barking noise she made.
I listened hard to make sure.

I heard a fox bark
in that voice. Maybe she was *thinking*
of a fox barking, long ago,
and that thinking CAME OUT LOUD.
If that's the way it worked.
I sat in shade
to listen.

Then there was just the sound
of her picking berries again.
Until her basket filled up.
And belly.

On the way home I heard CRICKET
noises. I heard a cricket
and turned over some stones
to find it. And a stump.
I couldn't find one.

Then I looked
at her. I should have known!
She got quiet as if I had lifted a stone off HER.

When I looked straight at her
she got quiet, yes, because that's how it goes
with a cricket
when its stone is lifted.

ALWAYS SURPRISED

Owls started this.

When this boy went owl looking
it was night. He would hear one
up ahead
and squint his eyes to try and see it.

He tried to catch one
by not making noise.

Then that owl called at him
from BEHIND!
And he jumped.

He only heard owls from behind.

Always fooled by owls,
which was, in later days, the cause
of his name. He got jumpy.
Even if a leaf fell on his shoulder
he jumped, JUMPED as if he was
always being surprised.

Or the first drop
of rain he felt, too,
he'd turn and say
"WHICH OWL SPIT THAT ON ME?"

Even in daylight.

WOKE INTO A HERON

She was tall, you could see her
in the distance before anyone.

Once, in late summer,
she stood so long at the edge
of the swamp
we thought she was ready
to leave with the herons.

You could see her standing
very still.

The day the herons left
she stayed. The next day she woke as a girl
all right, but she began being a HERON!
She took long steps, slowly, as if she was
walking in water, hunting in water.
This is true, and she did this
making heron noises.

AND had thin sticks
tied out from her feet
to make heron tracks.

This went away
the next morning. Everyone
was happy she would no longer
go sleep in the water reeds.

This was the first time we saw someone
do this, so we named her
not to forget it.

SAW THROUGH TO THE BOTTOM

There was a muddy lake no one dared
to fish in. It was close by,
but that didn't matter. Also, it was told
if we drank mud water into us
all we would want to do
is go far away and curl up
on some moss.

That was part of the trouble.

One other story about that lake
was that the giant mud fish
lived in it. And this sounded right, yes,
because we knew a mud fish
spoke out mud
into the water, OUT OF HIS MOUTH,
so he would always have a muddy place to swim.

So, this kept us away too.

One night this small girl went to sit
by the mud lake! She had a stick
and a rock, if the mud fish came after
her feet. She sat there a long time.
She stayed all night, and didn't sleep.
Then, she saw through to the bottom
of the lake, SAW THROUGH THE MUD ON TOP,
and what she saw were sturgeon
swimming down there.

She told us this.

Some of us believed her and went to catch
those sturgeon. This got known around
and, later, others lost their fear too.
After *our* babies got fat
on sturgeon.

QUIET UNTIL THE THAW

Her name tells of how
it was with her.

The truth is, she did not speak
in winter.
Everyone learned not to
ask her questions in winter,
once this was known about her.

The first winter this happened
we looked in her mouth to see
if something was frozen. Her tongue
maybe, or something else in there.

But after the thaw she spoke again
and told us it was fine for her that way.

So each spring we
looked forward to that.

WHO CALLED THE MUD-PLACES

I'll tell you
he would always be out front
when our families went walking.
He would step in the mud
before anyone else.

Then he would call
back to us, "MUD! MUD!"

And when he found some mud ahead of us
we would lift the new-walking babies
up on our shoulders
so they wouldn't get stuck
in mud.

Then, into the lake LAUGHING!
He washed that mud
off his feet. Sometimes he had
mud all over him!

He called the mud-places
each time we went walking.

So his name got on him
that way.

GOT DIZZY

This name happened
under hawks.
When he was young he stood
facing UP, watching hawks
fly in circles.

Those hawks would hunt in circles
and you could see him turn too,
trying to keep up.

So, then, by doing this
he made a hawk begin circling
inside his head and feet.
BOTH PLACES IN HIM GOT DIZZY!

Sometimes
he fell.

In the morning
when a hawk flew out of a cloud
or tree to hunt, he was waiting.

I believe he loved hawks
to make him dizzy this way.

Later on, he did a shouting game
to try and fool other kinds of birds
and mix them all up
into HAWKS.
He shouted, "Black Crow, turn in circles
in the sky!"

"Woodpecker, turn in circles
on the tree!"

But those other birds
knew what was going on.

TOOK HONEY WITH HIS FACE

He knew how bears got away
with it. He watched one
stick her nose deep in a hive
and get good honey on her face.

He knew this way
from watching.

So he dressed that way too,
with an old bear skin all over him
and mud-leaves on his face and hands
And stuck his face in a hive!

STUCK HIS FACE IN!

Got his feet stung.

But he got honey that way.

No one told him to use the wet
torch-stick smoke
to get out those bees.
No one told him this for a long time.
They liked watching his way
too much!

He took honey that way
a few times.

Then someone told him
how to use smoke.

Or he saw it done
from hiding.

SLAPPED THE WATER

This girl knew pond noises well,
beaver tail-slapping
and the sound of trees falling
into water
because of beavers.
You could find her footprints going
down to the pond, and sometimes see her
listening *in it* through a reed.
She must have heard
other water noises that way.
But I didn't ask.

I didn't ask about that, no,
but once I saw her slap the water
with her hand
and laugh. Later, I looked in her teeth
for bark chips!
Then we both laughed.

I don't think she ever did
any tree chewing though.

I didn't ask.

LISTENED TO BIRDS CRACK OUT

I'll tell what I know
about him.
One time he was there, RIGHT THERE,
when a bird egg cracked open
and one came out.
He heard that sound.

Then something
got into him. That sound got into him
and he wanted to hear every bird egg
crack open. EVERY ONE!

So he tried doing that
and ran from nest
to nest. He lay down with his ears
next to duck nests that were
in the reeds. Then he climbed
up to tree nests all over!

People saw him
at many places.

This went on.
He went looking for nest eggs
and later said he heard more
crack open.

He saved the shells
to remember how it went.

EYEBROWS MADE OF CROWS

If you looked hard enough CROWS were there
in those eyebrows that lived
on his forehead. Thick crow eyebrows, yes,
and when this boy yawned
those crows went UP,
then landed back down over his eyes.

When he began to get tired,
to yawn, the crows woke up more.

This happened when he laughed hard too.
One time joking stories were being told,
one after the other. This boy was laughing,
LAUGHING at each one. The crows
were rising and landing all the time
on his forehead. The harder the laughing got,
the higher those crows went.
We got worried they would fly away.
So we put maple-pitch
on those eyebrow crows,
to keep their feet stuck
home.

LARGER EARS

She had large ears, and this seemed
to please her. Even the time a man joked at her ears
and said they were BATS,
she chose to believe it! She said to him, "Yes,
you are right. They are bats!
I'm glad you came to tell me.
And I will send them into your house
THIS VERY NIGHT to hover
and listen over your face!"

This quickly stopped
his joking.

Also, she liked to listen to *large* sounds
with those large ears.
Maybe the two things
went together.
Before storms, she would sit along the edge
of a lake, EVEN AFTER IT BEGAN RAINING,
and listen to thunder.
Sometimes she shouted back
to it, "Louder, I can hardly hear you!"
Even though the rest of us
had our hands over our ears, as we sat
inside our houses.

Listening with our smaller ears.

TURNED WEEPING OVER

One time he came walking into the village
with a mossy-shell turtle
on the top of his head. He could balance things
that way, and it made us laugh.
Anyone who was weeping
and saw him with a basket on the end
of his thumb, or saw him do
some other kind of balancing,
got his weeping turned over by him
into laughing!

That time he walked in
with the mossy-shell turtle on his head,
everyone laughed!
Except the turtle.
That turtle had a straight face.

It was good to have him
in the village, that boy who did tricks
with his thumbs
and had the mossy-shell turtle
on the top of his head.
That one time.

DRIED THINGS OUT

One job she had was to dry fish
with smoke or in the sun,
and did this well. Some of her name
came from that.

Some days you could see her
stand in the water and find things
to dry there, too. Grasshoppers
or dragonflies the wind sent into the lake.

Or, they flew into the water themselves
because they saw clouds and high branches
reflected on the water
and thought they were flying UP
into the sky!

She would pick them up and hold them
in her hand, or put them
on a rock in the sun.
To dry their wings.

She would dry her wet skin, too,
sometimes with a dragonfly
on each knee.

All three drying in the sun.

Some of her name
came from that.

POLLEN LEGGINGS

She rolled in the flower fields.
That's one thing she did.
Sometimes pollen got all over her legs,
and they had the look
of yellow leggings.
LEGGINGS IN SUMMER!
That started us thinking of a name.

When she would come back to the village
one old woman always asked her,
"Do the flowers have pollen yet?"
This girl would sit down on a blanket,
then get up, leaving pollen from her legs
as the answer! It was a game
those two did just among themselves.

That went on, too.

Pollen leggings, yes. We saw the chance
to hear a winter *and* summer thing
in a name.
So we didn't let that pass by.

WHO TAPPED THE FROGS IN

First thing to know is
he was blind
so he walked along the stream
a different way.

He had a long stick and made his way
with it.

Frogs sat along the bank
listening and singing at the same time
until they heard that stick coming near
on the ground. Then each frog
jumped in!

And that's how this boy knew
where the water was, by the sound
those frogs made jumping in.
Now you know.

He followed the stream
out and back.

Keeping his feet dry that way.

All along the edge.

LEANED OVER

One night he tied a moose skull WITH ANTLERS
on his head, and tried to frighten us
with it. He leaned over a cliff above us.
He made loud moose noises! Then we heard
the first stones fall. Everyone scattered.

He had leaned over too far!
We saw him stuck
halfway down the cliff.

On our way to get him we spoke
of how we looked forward
to eating THIS MOOSE STUCK UP THERE,
and how we could almost smell the meat
on the fire.

"Let's cook it right away!" I heard.

He heard this too, and quickly tried
to get out of the vines
he was stuck in.
We got closer,
saying how hungry we were.

That's when he shouted LOUD,
in a human voice
this time.
He shouted that he wasn't a moose.

But we began talking the way
moose talk, in throat echoes.
Grunting, and making moose calls!

He must have thought
the moose of all the lakes
were after him! He shouted, "I'm on
the other, far side of the cliff, moose!"
He tried that.

But we knew
where he was.

We got closer, and he saw us.
But we did not rescue him
right away. We stood talking
about how disappointed we were
THAT HE WASN'T A MOOSE.
How we were tricked.

"Let's go look for moose, then!"
someone said. It was agreed on.

We began to leave, which is when
he began making promises
not to frighten us, from then on.

Then, we got him down
from the cliff.

WHO HEARD SQUIRRELS

He would just stop in the middle
of talking, if he heard
squirrel noises.

And, he knew which tree to wait under
for squirrels. Even if he went out
in the dark
he knew which tree was going to be loud
before the squirrels got there!

I always remember this out loud
to people too: He would stop paddling
out near the center of a fishing lake,
to listen. Quietly. He would say nothing,
just chew on his knuckles
with his teeth
to show me he heard a squirrel.

I knew he wished his knuckles
were walnuts!

That far out in the lake I could hear
the paddles drip water all right,
but no squirrel noises!

But I saw a squirrel wake up
in *his* face, each time this happened.

SAW THE CLOUD LYNX

There was a boy in a village who made
wood stilts. Yes, he saw them made somewhere
and learned how. He spent a long time
knife whittling
and when he was finished
he walked on those stilts to the lake.
Walked around the shallows,
being tall.
Soon, others arrived to hunt fish
and he was UP IN THE AIR pointing out fish
to them.

He walked around with trees
for legs.

While he was up in the air he looked
far off in the distance
and saw a strange thing happen.
He saw a round cloud
grow an ear!
Then, it grew another ear!
He knew the wind did things such as this
to clouds, so he kept it to himself.
At first.

Then those ears
had a face between them.
It was
a lynx face!

The face was blowing toward THE LAKE
WHERE THEY WERE! He knew that giant lynx
would be coming toward them faster

as soon as it got the wind
to grow it legs.

That's when he told the others.

They ran, ha!
All the young ones!

Those wood stilts
stood STRAIGHT UP in mud
until he went back to get them.
After the sky cleared.

CHANGED HIS MIND

One night we were ready to put out
the central fire, when he walked up
and said, "Watch, I'll put it out
with my hands!" We stood back.
Then, instead of using his hands
he threw some wet leaves on the fire
and stomped on it until it was out.
Thick smoke went up in front of us,
so we did not see him disappear.

The next day we asked him
about this, and he just said,
"Wet leaves and feet
are better
for putting fires out."

That was one time.

Later, we had to make a tree bridge
across a ravine. Many of us lifted a fallen tree
and let it fall again across the ravine.
That's when he appeared
and said, "Watch, I'll test this bridge
by walking across it on my hands!"
He walked on his hands to begin with
all right, but when he neared the tree
he quickly stood up again and ran across it.
ON HIS FEET! He didn't look back at us.

The next day we asked him
about *this*, and he just seemed
sad.
He said, "Feet are better for that."

There was another time, too,
when we saw a snapping turtle
sitting on a log. He said, "I'll catch it
with my hands!"
Then, he began wading into the water
toward that turtle. He had his hands ready.
When he got close, the turtle
turned and looked right at him
WITH ITS MOUTH OPEN!
The boy splashed out to dry land, and
ran out saying, "Feet are better for this!"

He walked on his feet
home.

FAR NORTH BEAST
GHOSTS THE CLEARING:
Short Poems

S HORT poems, like the ones translated in this chapter, may be spoken by anyone in a Cree community. Once told, even poems derived from the most personal experiences become community property. This process of assimilation allows for endless variation on an original theme. Thomas Johns Bear, a fine Cree teller, told me: "I tell poems to a small pond first. I only tell them in summer. I throw a rock in. The circles go out from where it hits. Then I say, 'Water, you stutter! Water, calm down!' Then I tell a poem to calm it down. Later I bring it to other people and tell it to them. Each of us does it differently."

I heard these poems during conversations, ceremonies, and exchanges of stories in which I participated. The birth songs I heard in homes. They were sung to each child by his or her father, as well as for the benefit of gathered family and friends, who often accompanied the songs with the music of rattles.

Group exchanges of stories tend to involve poems told in the style of the older, much longer tales. Examples of these are the poems beginning "I never saw Wolverine" and "I wanted to travel with the porcupine," both of which feature dialogue, specific episodes, and the long timespans common to tales generally. John Rains once said: "Poems are told all the time. I'll complain one to you"—a statement he followed with:

> I am the poorest one.
> I cook bark.
> I have bad luck in hunting.
> A duck caught my arrow
> and used it
> for her nest.

93

I am the poorest one.
I sit in mud and weep.
I have bad luck in hunting.
A goose caught my arrow
and broke it
in two.

I am old, old.
Don't bring me pity,
but food
yes.

That far north beast
there, with icicle shag hair
hanging down.
That beast winter sits on.

You'll see him
ghost the clearing.
Snow falls on him, then
snow stops falling
and he's a pile of snow!
Eyes showing through,
ears shivering snow off,
whole body shaking snow,
snow flying around him.
So it snows off him.
So it does.

With you I want to carve
the owl stick.
With your help
we'll carve it.

The crow stick failed.
So what.
The duck stick failed.
So what.

This is different.
This time.

They'll see it fly, owl.
They'll hear it call, owl.
They'll say "Owl stick lives nearby."

And they'll stop gossiping
about those two old ones
always carving, night and day.

You don't believe it?
I'll prove it,
that shadows have thickness!
Here's the spot, out in the sun.

These were brought here
from all over,
in arms, on dog sleds,
flew in the wind too.
All to get here
piled up.

Come on, tell me,
is that a pile of shadows
or not?

Shadow of the blue eggs
in there,
and the nest
and the jay who came
to rob it all.

And that's just one
shadow-story.
It'll take you maybe five days
of your life
to count all the stories
stacked up here.
Better start now.

Skeleton of a bear,
white bones,
went and rolled in some mud.
The mud stuck on
but rain
washed his body away.

Skeleton of a bear,
white bones,
went and rolled in some ashes.
The ashes stuck on
but wind
blew his body away.

Skeleton of a bear,
who weeps for him?

Look at him,
all alone,
white bones
without a coat.

Look at me
living here alone
between two villages.
Why was I born here
between two villages?

Yes,
I visit each village
but I always come back here,
between.
And I know how to weep for those bear bones

in their loneliness.
I know how to weep for those bear bones
in their shivering.
But I'll go on wearing
his old coat that I hunted
over me
these cold nights.

Things that wash up
I live in.
Old dead reeds
wash up
at the edge
of the lake.
I curl up in them.
I live in them awhile.

I can do this.
I've no fear of this.

The shells
that wash up
in the river.
No snails in them.
All cleaned out by the water
tumbling.
I live in them awhile.

Anything.
All things.
Things that wash up
I live in.

So now I go walking
with the sounds of water
in my ears.
Little creek sound.
Swift river sound.
The sound of waves on a lake.
I walk toward them.

Oh wash up new things
for me to live in!

Owl.
Top of the pine owl.
That's not your body below you.

Do you think
your feathers are green needles?
Do you think
your bones are tree wood?
Do you think
a mouse couldn't hear you
miles away
as you came crashing through the forest
chasing after it,
if your body was that whole pine tree?

Owl.
Owl sitting on top of the pine.
Rise up and see!
It's better the way you are.

The goose is frozen in the lake.
I'm going to thaw it out.

The goose was hurt in the wings.
The ice came fast.
The others left without it.
The ice came fast.

I'll build a small fire
by the goose.
Frightened look in its eyes.
See, its neck is stretching
the way the others went.
It's got the south
in its neck,
stretching that way.
But the wings kept it here.
The broken wings.

I'm going to thaw it out.

Old jay, loudmouth of the tree!
Tell me the news.
What's that,
the lightning put a scar
on your tree?
"Crooked lightning, crooked scar!"
you call down
to me.

Old man crooked
from my village
goes walking.
Old man, bent over,
moves his hand
over the scar
on your tree.
Old jay, loudmouth,
tell him the news.
"There's crooked lightning in your back!"
you call down
to him.
Old jay, loudmouth
knows it.

Now we are outside
in spring!

These people who made it
through winter
sit together and talk.
See them!
They have many stories.
They rub their hands
over a fire
and sing "We rub hands.
          We rub winter out
          of our hands."

Now we are outside
in spring!

These people who made it
through winter
walk together.
See them!
They stop to rub their feet
and put them
on each other's bellies
for the warmth there.
They sing "We rub feet.
          We rub winter out
          of our feet."

This happens
each spring.

In my illness I saw a man born
out of a hive.
He flew
to work among flowers,
he had wings,
he was invisible sometimes
in the sun,
he did not know my face.
I saw him in my fever.
It was me I saw.

In my illness
gone on another day
I saw a man born
in a nest of rabbits.
He was left alone.
He was shivering in the sight
of many fireflies
in the woods.
The fireflies were the eyes
of floating wolves.
In my illness they were hungry.
In my fever it was me
they looked at.

In my illness
almost gone this day,
I remember these things.

So you came to surprise me
again today, wind!
First you tossed me down.
Then you brought rain in from somewhere
to soak my clothes
drying over a fire
while I slept.
Later you sent the smell
of my good deer liver
to the wasps
in one of your breezes.
They came and settled on it awhile.
Do you think I could get near it?
If I could find your legs I'd tie them.
If I could find your face I'd snap at it.
If I could find your hair I'd hire some lice.
All on this day,
wind!

I bind a long stick
to the shore
of the lake.
It's a long handle to the lake.
It's a long handle to the old spoon.

Lake, hollow spoon
before the rains filled you.
At the beginning
of the world
you were a giant hollow spoon.

Now we need the water.
We use it
in all seasons.
We bathe in it.
We float canoes on it.
We fish through the ice.
We see the moon on it.
All these things to do
in the spoon.

Take a little water
for broth.
Plenty of water for broth.

I bind a long stick
to the shore
of the lake.
It's a long handle to the lake.
It's a long handle to the old spoon.

A small lynx
lost his family.
He went out on his own
and began learning things.
He just set out.

One spring he saw
birds arrive
from the south.
He tasted some.
He learned those tastes.

One summer he nearly
drowned, but he saw his face
a long time
in that lake.
He learned his face then.

One autumn he was as big
as his parents,
and this made him think
about them.
That's how he learned
to remember.

Once, in the cold of winter,
he found an ice bird
who did not move.
That's how he learned weeping,
all down his face,
onto that bird.
He bent over it a long time.

I know his story,

what he learned.
I know it.
I tell it to you.
All these things!
I weep when I tell it.
I am Small Lynx.

I wake and see my wife.
My eyes are all right
another day!
So I go out looking.
I go out looking
for a quiet lake
to fish in.
I go out looking.
But the wind is hard
over all the lakes.
Wind swirling branches
into the water.
Wind howling
and birds trying to fly home
in it.
I go home too.
My eyes are good this day.
I find my way home.

I hear the wind in the far distance.
My ears are good another day!

I see the birds trying hard to get home
My eyes are good another day!

I smell the cooking fire outside.
My nose is good another day!

On this day that I stay home.

I'm in trouble swimming
in my shirt
made of moss.
I'm in big trouble
in this shirt.
The water was too cold.
I wanted to stay warm in my shirt.
The water soaks in!
The moss is drinking.
Stop drinking, moss!

Wait until summer to swim
you told me.

But I didn't listen.

Now I'm in big trouble
going under
in my shirt
made of moss.

If I had such cleverness
I would put thunder
in the ears
of my enemy
and lightning in his eyes
He would not be able
to find the way
to the place I live.

If I had such cleverness
I would tie my enemy
to the tail
of an otter sliding forever
in snow and mud.
No fighting this way.
I'd stay home.

If I knew how,
my sleeping
would be the grunts
of bears.
Those bears would fly out
and find my enemy,
and my enemy
would be stealing their berries.
I wouldn't hear a thing that went on

I'd be sleeping
far away.

The trees are creaking
in the wind.
The truth of it is
I am afraid this night
because it is the hardest wind
of my life.

I want to float out on the lake
in case a tree falls.
I want to fly above
in case it falls.
I want to go and sleep in a cave.
The tree could never
break through the rock
it has for a roof!

All this night
the creaking of trees.

Land of old men
Land of old women
moaning in those trees.

Maybe my own grandparents
in one.

All this night
the creaking of trees,
all through it
I stay awake.

I stay awake.

I am the poorest one.
I cook bark.
I have bad luck in hunting.
A duck caught my arrow
and used it
for her nest.

I am the poorest one.
I sit in mud and weep.
I have bad luck in hunting.
A goose caught my arrow
and broke it
in two.

I am old, old.
Don't bring me pity,
but food
yes.

That man!
That one whose fire
sends up only fog,
lives here.

There!
Fog rising above the trees.
It's him.

There he is, feeding sticks
to his fire.
Fog rises up instead of smoke.
Only his fire does this.

One time I was looking
at the knotholes of trees.
That's what they were,
knotholes.
Then he came along
and built his fire
among those trees.
The fog began rising!
All through the trees.
All around them.
Then the knotholes came out
of the fog at me.
I saw them differently.
Now they were faces.
Faces of seals.
Faces of foxes.
Many animal faces.

I saw those faces
because of him, that man
who causes fog.

Try to catch him,
he builds a fire.

Try to catch him,
the fog gets thick
around him.

Try to catch him,
and he's gone.

He's the one.

I wanted to travel with the porcupine.
He said, "No, you're too thin.
You're like an aspen stick!
The others would laugh at me
and say, *'Gnaw the bark off him
and go on walking.'* "
That's all he had to say to me.

So, I ate all day.
I did this five days.
The first day I got sick,
then I was all right.
And I was fat!

When I saw the porcupine again
he said, "Well, you're fat enough,
but your back is too smooth."
So I tied sticks
all over me.

Then he said, "That's good,
but now you have to learn
to be alone. Go climb up those rocks
and live in a cave some days.
I did that.
I lived alone in there many days and nights.
I talked to myself.
I sang to myself.
I was so lonely I would have
married the first thing
that came into the cave!
Then the porcupine said, "Come out."

For a long time after that
we travelled together.

I never saw Wolverine
but I knew of his cleverness.
I wanted to meet him,
tricky one, clever one.

But every one said,
"He'll never come and talk with you."

I tried to figure out
a way.

So, I started saying bad things
about him, rotten things,
all lies.
I said, "Wolverine shits out whole hills."
The next day my house was covered.

Then I said, "Wolverine sneaks up on people."
When I got home my wife was gone.

Then I shut up
because everything I said
about him turned true.

Well, one day he showed up.
We spoke at each other.
I said, "You're rotten.
You're a thief!"
He said, "Oh don't be angry.
Let's be friends. I've changed
for the better. I'll get you a new wife."

"Will she be fat?" I asked.

"No," he said.

All this talk confused me.
I almost did not want
to jump on him anymore
and fight.
Suddenly, he threw off his face
and fur skin. It was my wife!
"Wolverine sent me! Ha!" she said.
Then she ran back
into the woods forever.

The truth is
I have mud on my hands
from digging roots

The truth is
I brought them to you

It is the truth
I worked to get them
and complained
while digging them up

The truth is
once I got back here
and saw your face
it didn't matter,

that work

Little snail
curled up

leaving a snail shape
in the blanket

when I lift you

If I popped out of the snow
with ten crows
tied to the top
of my head

you still would not wake

deepest sleeping one
I've ever seen

I'm no owl
don't you believe it

Just because my big
feather face
is so round
looking over yours
when you wake,
don't believe
I'll fly away
in the morning!

There's things I do
There's things I do

in happiness
of your arrival

Today I was out
stooping my shoulders
in the lily-pad water
with moose

O-HA!

so happy
it was all I could think
to do

Crow
sit down
shut up

can't you see
who's sleeping?

It's her
just born and not ready
to hear your crow noises yet

Sit down
shut up

I can't travel
away from you

rolling pine cone

Each time I go to leave
my shoes hide
in your dreams

All the warm nights
sleep in moonlight

keep letting it
go into you

do this
all your life

do this
you will shine outward
in old age

the moon will think
you are
the moon

Wild turkeys
dance
on a mound of earth

and the moles
under them
say
"We know the earth
is loud
with turkeys again"

But you,
not-yet-born,
when I tap my fingers
on the mound over you

do you know who dances?

Old turtle
walked this far
to see

Who-woke-up-here

I'll pick you up
to see

Well,
here she is

wrinkled as you are

WICHIKAPACHE GOES WALKING, WALKING:
A Tale

*T*HE *narrative translated here is one of the atayoh-kāwin (this is more or less precisely a Plains Cree phonetic spelling), or "sacred stories," concerned with a time when primarily totem ancestors and the Crees' creator-trickster figure, Wichikäpache, roamed the earth. In this tale one can see how Wichikäpache continually reaffirms his creator role by shouting phrases such as "I MADE THIS WORLD!" and how other characters do the same by addressing him as "Elder Brother." It may be generally said that Wichikäpache is a powerful character figure among the more eastern Algonquian groups, though certainly he is an omnipresent, illustrious figure having great inventive powers throughout the Algonquian world.*

This translation is from a performance by Jacob Nibènegenesábe, on July 26, 1969, near Kiskito Lake, Manitoba. The performance was witnessed by about ten persons—all, except for myself, Cree.

In keeping with Nibènegenesábe's style of telling, words spoken loudly are here represented by capital letters, and those spoken softly by italics. Traditionally, Wichikäpache's name is often spoken loudly in tales, twice in a row, reaffirming the fact that a sacred story is in progress. In my translation of Nibènegenesábe's telling, line breaks represent normal pauses in speech. The lines of three spaced periods, which generally follow the phrase He went walking *(or a variation on that), indicate a much longer passage of time. These longer pauses, among Cree tellers, are often used for focused, dramatic effect. For instance, after* Wichikäpache *assigns the weasel who helped him its winter and summer colors, it is said:*

Wichikapache

•   •   •

went walking

"With all *Wichikäpache's walking, I get tired*," *Nibène-genesábe stated after the tale. The active performance certainly exhausted many who participated in the listening. Some persons let out deep sighing breaths and slumped their shoulders when the tale was completed. Wichikäpache is always moving, even in sleep:*

In his dream
he went walking.

Nutoka moo
Usa puyew usu wapiw

WICHIKAPACHE
packed up his few carrying things
and went walking. As he walked, he heard *animal noises.*
Animal noises,
all around.
Then, up ahead, he saw a moose deer
sloshing around in a marsh.
When the moose saw him
it began running.
"Wait a minute," Wichikapache said, "Little Brother,
don't run. Let's talk!"
Let's talk, yes, that's what he said.

The moose stopped
and looked at him,
with great suspicion the moose looked at him.
It got quiet.
THE BIRDS STOPPED TALKING.
The squirrels stopped talking.
All the animals watched.
They watched.
Then, Wichikapache said, "Listen,
I've got troubles. I weep a lot lately.
My face swells up. Don't you feel pity for me?
It's my sorrow I tell you about."

"What can I do
to help?"
the moose said.

"Just come over here. Over here,
and give me some sympathy,"

135

Wichikapache said.

The moose approached *carefully*,
but not careful
in its thinking.

"Why
you're all hot from running," Wichikapache said.
He touched the moose's belly.

THEN,
he stabbed the moose
with a knife.
The moose died with this trick in its eyes.
It was Wichikapache's trick
and it worked.

Well then,
he cut up the moose.
This was done then.
He cut it up into pieces.
He would eat some, and save some.
For later.
He cracked the bones
to get marrow.
Then,
he put the marrow fat inside a bag
made out of the bladder.

It was all done, then.
It was all done in a short time.

Wichikapache went
to the river.
He saw muskrats there.

They were swimming and eating.
He called to them, "Come here!
One of you, I need some help."

One swam over to him.
He said, "Muskrat, I want this marrow fat cooled.
I want it cooled in the water."
He tied the bag of it
to the tail
of the muskrat.
He watched the muskrat swim away,
trailing the bag of marrow.

Out in the water
the muskrat called back to Wichikapache,
"Don't frighten me now!
I know of your tricks.
So,
if you want this fat cooled properly,
leave me alone.
The work will get done."

Wichikapache watched from shore.
Then
he tied a bush to the top of his head,
covered his face with mud
and leaped out!
He shouted "SSSSSSSS AAAAGHH!"
The muskrat's heart flew up into his throat!
The muskrat swam
in circles.
He splashed and cried out
and spilled the marrow fat
It floated on the water.
Wichikapache jumped in

and began lapping it up.
"Men will call this stuff FOAM!"
he said.
"I'll get back to you later, muskrat."
Then
he swam to shore.

He went walking.

•　　•　　•

It became winter then.
The forest
was covered with snow.
Ahead,
he saw some huts.
Children were playing around them.
He called to one, "Come here Little Brother
I need your help."
The child came over.
"Tell me,
where is the head man's hut?
Which one is it?"
The child pointed at one.
Wichikapache went to it and walked in.

The man inside said, "Welcome,
sit down."
He was given some food.

"Don't get too comfortable,"
the man said.
"We move around a lot.
We've moved four times in the last five days
In fact,
in the morning we'll move again."

But
Wichikapache undressed.
He took his clothes off
and hung them
over the fire to dry
from wet snow.
Smoke went into them.
Then
he lay down and fell asleep.

In his dream
he went walking.

● ● ●

In the morning
many ptarmigan flew up into the air!
Wichikapache found himself
lying on snow!
It was freezing cold.
His clothes
hung on the tree.
They looked like shirt
and pants
and coat icicles.
He built a fire under them
to turn them back into clothes.
WICHIKAPACHE ALMOST FROZE TO DEATH!
Those ptarmigan
had moved on!
He forgot he was warned
and got angry.

He shouted, "I MADE THIS WORLD.
I'LL FIND THOSE PTARMIGAN
AND TAKE CARE OF THEM!"

Then
he went walking.

•　　•　　•

He walked all winter.
Some said they saw him
living in trees,
under the ice,
and once
he poked his head out
of an owl nest.

•　　•　　•

Then
it was spring.
He was out walking again.
He came upon some young ptarmigan
in their nest.
"What do you go by?"
he asked them.

There was no answer.

"What do you go by, ptarmigan?"
he asked again.

"YOU JUST SAID IT,"
they answered.

"Yes,
but most things
get at least two names,"

Wichikapache said.
"For instance,
BORN OF OLD,
which is me."

Then
the ptarmigan said, "O.K.
we're called
FAT MUD FACES."

"NO!" Wichikapache said,
"You joke me."

"You're right," the ptarmigan said,
"Really
we are called MANY TOAD FEET."

"No, you still joke me,"
Wichikapache said.

"Very well,
you see through us.
We are called SMALL WINGED STARTLERS,"
the ptarmigan said.

Just then
another group of ptarmigan flew up,
making a lot of noise.
WICHIKAPACHE'S HEART
flew up
into his mouth.
He remembered the muskrat.

"You see now,"
the ptarmigan said,

"in truth
that is what we're called."

Wichikapache felt tricked.
and began to think.
His fast breathing
made his heart
join in on the thinking.
Then
he shit on the ptarmigan's nest.
Now you know
what he was thinking about.

He went walking.

● ● ●

Soon the older ptarmigan came home
to find their young
with shit on their feathers.
All over
the feathers.
The ptarmigan grew angry.
Some of them set out
to find Wichikapache.
They waited for him
by a stream.
"Talk only to your own stomachs,"
one said.
"That way
Wichikapache won't hear you."
They waited.

● ● ●

WICHIKAPACHE
came walking along.
He saw
the stream.
He leaned over to drink.
Then
he stood up
and shouted, "I'LL RUN AT THIS STREAM
FOUR TIMES!
THEN I'LL LEAP ACROSS IT!"

He backed up
and ran toward the stream.
Just before he got to it
he stopped.
The ptarmigan were watching
talking to their stomachs.
They were puzzled.
Well then,
Wichikapache did the same thing
three more times.
Then
he said, "NOW I've done that four times.
NOW
I leap across!"
He tried it,
and fell in.
FELL IN!
and began floating down the stream.
All his carrying things
were lost.
Floating
and tumbling away
they went.
WICHIKAPACHE

managed to get to shore.
He had lost everything.
Shells, meat, everything.
He dove back in the stream
to look for things.
His things
and whatever else he might find.
He looked in the stream
all day,
with no luck.
Then,
THEN he saw his things
hanging from a branch.
"AGH!
SOMEONE DID THIS TO ME!"
He got out of the stream.

He walked away from there.

● ● ●

While walking
he came upon a lake.
Ducks
were in it.
"Elder Brother," one called,
"What is that
you have on your back?"

Wichikapache said,
"The shut-eye dance."

"Show us then,"
the duck said.

"It's very difficult,"
Wichikapache said.

"Let us try it at least,"
the duck said.

"All right."
All right
Wichikapache said.
Then
Wichikapache built a dance lodge.
He gathered
many ducks
to dance.
They were ready.

"You must shut your eyes
for this dance,"
Wichikapache said.
"You must,"
is what he said.

Then
he began to sing.

The ducks danced
with their eyes closed.

Then,   THEN   And some say it was because
he thought the ducks had taken his clothes.
He began
killing the ducks.
I say
he was hungry too.

That was another thing here.
He killed a lot of them.
But a few had only one eye closed
because they had heard of Wichikapache's tricks
as they danced
these few had only one eye closed.
One of these shouted, "He's killing us!"
Some got away,
the diver duck
and one with a mask on.

WICHIKAPACHE
Wichikapache said, "I didn't have any dance!"
He said
he was hungry
and angry.
But
there was no one left to listen to him.

He began
to cook the ducks.
They were cooking on a fire.
So
he went walking.

•   •   •

Outside
he ran into a fox.
"Ho! Little Brother,
let's race.
Let's race
and whoever wins
gets to eat all the ducks.
What do you say?"

146

The fox said, "No, I have
a bad leg.
And
the wind put a knot in my tail,
so I am unbalanced."

"O.K. then," Wichikapache said,
"I'll tie some rocks
to my leg."

"That's fair enough," the fox said.
Fair enough
he said.

WICHIKAPACHE
tied rocks to his leg.
They began racing.
Wichikapache was going slow
because of the rocks.
The fox was limping along
and his tail was flopping from one side
over
to the other,
flopping.
They ran toward a hill,
and each of them
went a different way around it.
As soon as the fox is out of sight,
out of Wichikapache's sight,
he untied the knot in his tail
and ran well again.
He ran straight back to the ducks
racing with his nose
the way there
and quickly ate them.

147

He ate everything
except for the feet and bills.

Except
for those.

•   •   •

That night,
it took him until night

Wichikapache arrived there.

He pulled one duck
out of the ashes.
"I cooked him too long," he said.
He pulled
ALL the duck feet and bills
out of the ashes.
"I COOKED THEM ALL TOO LONG!"

THEN,   *then*
he understood.

He called out loud, "I MADE THIS WORLD
FOX,
I'LL FIND YOU!"

He went walking.

Looking.

•   •   •

And

he found the fox sleeping
and fat.
Wichikapache tried to think what to do.
He thought to himself,
"If I club him
I'll bruise the fur.
And I want it for a carrying pouch.
Well,
I'd better build a fire,
and let smoke go into his nose and mouth."

So
he set fire to sticks
around the fox.
The fox leaped awake!
He was encircled by fire.

"Ha!
You can't escape, fox!
You who ate all my ducks.
You who tricked me
and snuck back
to do some duck eating!"

Then
smoke went up all around.
When it subsided
there was no fox.
He had escaped.

"Where did you go
duck-breath thief?"
Wichikapache shouted.
"WHO DO YOU THINK MADE THIS WORLD?"

He went walking.

•   •   •

While he was out walking
he came upon some jays.
The jays
were pulling their eyes out
and juggling them.
The eyes flew up
and were caught.
Then
the jays tossed their eyes up
into some bushes.
They shook the bushes
and the eyes
flew back into place
in their faces.

"What's the reason,
WHAT IS THE REASON FOR THIS?"
Wichikapache asked them.

"We
have headaches,"
one jay said.
"This cures it."

"Yes?"
Wichikapache said,
"well, then show me how
because I have a bad headache."

"It's very difficult,"
a jay said.

"Please
show me.

150

I have this bad pain in my head.
At least ten woodpeckers are inside it."

"All right,"
one jay said.
And he gave Wichikapache
four doses of a medicine.
This gave him the power
to pull out his eyes.

Wichikapache
went walking.

•   •   •

Soon
his headache got worse.
He said, "Awgh!
My head   *my head inside it.*
More woodpeckers
got in somehow."
He stepped into the bushes
and began juggling his eyes.
Then
he tossed his eyes up
into some bushes.
When he shook the bushes
his eyes fell back into place
in his head.
His headache was gone.
It was gone.

He began walking.

•   •   •

But soon
the headache returned.
It was worse than before.
He said, "Awgh! *woodpeckers.*"
Again he went into the bushes.
Again
he tossed up his eyes.
Again they stuck in the bushes.
All this went as before.
But
when he tugged at the bushes this time
his eyes were gone!
The fox had stolen his eyes.
He didn't know this at first,
WICHIKAPACHE *didn't know who it was.*
He kept tugging at the bushes
all day.
All day he tugged at them.
Now he was blind.

He went walking.

•   •   •

The fox saw him
and came up
and poked him in the eye sockets!
With a stick
he did that.
HE DID THAT!

"Oh no!"
Wichikapache said,
"I keep running
into low branches."

Then the fox
left him alone.

As he walked on
again he bumped into something.
"Are you a tree?"

"If so
what kind?"
Wichikapache asked.

"I'm a birch,"
was the answer.

"Not the kind I want,"
Wichikapache said.
He walked on.

He bumped into a tree.
"What kind are you?"
he asked it.

"A spruce,"
was the answer.

"Good.
You're the kind I want."
Wichikapache
rubbed his hands over the tree
to find spruce resin.
He found it
and put some in his eye sockets.
Those
were his eyes now.

Then he said, "I know it was the fox
who poked me in the eye sockets.
It took me a while to figure it out.
It took me a while.
Now, I'LL FIND YOU, FOX,
AND TAKE CARE OF YOU!"

He began

•   •   •

walking.

•   •   •

He walked
a long time.

Finally he heard the sound of a dance.
He stopped walking to hear it
clearly.
It was a goose dance.
Sure enough
some people were dressed in goose feathers
and walking around in a squat position.
Making goose noises.
How they looked like geese!
It was the dance of the goose walk.
Just then
Wichikapache saw the head of a deer.
It was lying on the ground.
It had flies on it.
The flies were busy
and Wichikapache admired them for their busyness.
"Little Brothers,

154

little little brothers," he said,
"I will become a fly now."

"It's difficult,"
one fly said.

"Let me be one," Wichikapache said.

"All right,"
one fly said,
"our Elder Brother
will become a small fly."

"NO!" Wichikapache said,
"A LARGE FLY!"

"No, please be satisfied
with being a small fly,"
one said.

"All right," Wichikapache said.

So
he became a fly.

THEN
quite suddenly he TURNED BACK INTO A HUMAN
SHAPE
and grabbed the whole deer head for himself.
He fastened it
over his own head
and went off.
He went slow because of the weight.
The deer head was over his own.

Again,
so again
he was blind.

Still
he walked along.

He came upon a stream,
tripped
and rolled in.
The water swirled him along.
He went over rocks.

Soon
the people who owned the deer head
went after it.

They saw it floating by in the stream!

One old woman took a heavy club
and went for the deer floating by.
One old man was going to whistle loud
in the deer's ears!
One young man said, "GET THAT DEER FLOATING
BY!"
Wichikapache got out of the stream
but tripped again
and fell against some rocks.
The club woman came running.
The whistling man came running.
But
the deer head had fallen off.
The old woman called out, "Ha!
It's only Wichikapache!"
They all were laughing.

They all laughed hard,
which gave him time to get away.
He went running.

•　　•　　•

He came upon some geese.
He said, "Little Brothers,
make me a goose!"
"Too difficult," one said.

"No,
do this for me,"
Wichikapache said.

Do this for me
he said.

"All right,"
one goose said.

Then
Wichikapache was a goose.
He received these instructions:
"WHENEVER YOU SEE PEOPLE, FLY."

Then they all ate in the lake.
They dove,
tails went up in the air.
They rattled teeth,
and talked.

Then
they flew up into the air.

Wichikapache looked for people.
Just to be difficult.
Just to be contrary he did this.
He saw some.
The other geese worried and fled.
But Wichikapache,
WICHIKAPACHE flew LOWER
and invited arrows into him.
The arrows flew up at him.
WICHIKAPACHE
started doing tricks in the air.
The arrows hit the air around him,
but missed Wichikapache.
Then
with all his twists and turns
he burst the goose skin!
IT BURST!
An old woman looked up
and said, "Ha! It's Wichikapache again!"
They stopped shooting arrows.

Then
he left that place.

He was hungry.

He went walking.

•   •   •

He was very hungry.

He came upon some skunks
who were carrying out a wrestling match
with their tails.

No, I can't eat skunks, Wichikapache thought to himself.
Then
he said out loud,
"No,
but I'll use them!"

"Ho!
Little Brothers,
how are you?"

When they saw who it was
the skunks kept wrestling.
They wanted no part of him.
They kept busy.

"I don't mean to disturb you,"
Wichikapache said,
"but I've made a big decision.
I want to be a skunk.
You seem to be the best animals.
Let me become a skunk.
I've thought about it."

"It's too difficult,"
one skunk told him.

"No,
I know I can do it,"
Wichikapache said.

A skunk then said,

"You must realize
that you will receive strange reactions
from the others around here."

"Yes, I know,"
he said.
Yes I know this, Wichikapache said.

Then, THEN Wichikapache
became a skunk.

He walked over to some deer.
The deer plugged their noses
with weeds
but otherwise did nothing.
"Hello deer,"
he said.

"Hello skunk,"
the deer answered.

Then Wichikapache CHANGED BACK,
he changed back into a human shape,
leaped on one deer and killed it.
He had it planned out.

He sat down to eat.

When he was done
he went walking.

Again.

. . .

This time
he came upon a cabin.
A poorly built cabin.
Wichikapache heard howling noises inside.
Howling noises.
He sat down to listen.
The noises went on.
He got curious and approached
the house
he approached.
He looked in
and saw a Windigo
looking in a mirror.
A
Windigo.
Then
he heard the Windigo say
into the mirror,
"I am quite beautiful really.
I've been wasting my time.
I've wasted my skills,
eating meat all the time.
I'll throw out my cache of meat!"

Then,
just then,
she threw out her supply of meat.

WICHIKAPACHE RAN,
he ran away.

The Windigo looked back in the mirror
and saw an ugly face,
frightening it was.

161

A frightening face.
"Wichikapache did this!"

The Windigo went out.
She went after Wichikapache.

•   •   •

When she caught him,
she said, "Get some sticks,
Wichikapache,
plenty of them."

WICHIKAPACHE
had to do this.
He gathered sticks.
He wept as he did this
because he knew the fire was to be for him.

Sure enough,
the Windigo
was building a cooking fire.

"Go get more sticks.
More!"
the Windigo said.

While he was gathering sticks
Wichikapache saw a weasel.
A weasel, he thought.
"Oh Little Brother,
please
come here,"
Wichikapache said.

"No!
You'll hurt me,"
the weasel said.

Then Wichikapache wept.
Wept,
wept.
"The thing is," he said,
"a Windigo
is going to kill me.
Try and do something to her.
If you do,
I'll fix it so you are beautiful."

"All right,"
the weasel said.

Then,
the weasel left.

•　　•　　•

The weasel went walking.

•　　•　　•

The weasel found the Windigo.
It slipped
into her mouth,
crawled down her throat,

and bit her heart!
Her *heart.*

The Windigo called out to Wichikapache,

163

"Hurry with those sticks.
With all this waiting,
I've got a strange feeling inside me."

So Wichikapache went to her.
The Windigo,
feeling then she was dying,
clawed at Wichikapache.
She grabbed him.
THEY BOTH SCREAMED!
There was
screaming.
But when she died
Wichikapache was the only one still screaming.

The weasel
had done the job well.

"Thanks Little Brother,"
Wichikapache said.
"AND NOW,
now
in winter you will be white,
and your tail
will have a black tip on it.
And in summer
you will be brown
but your tail
will remain black.
Now, I leave.

Wichikapache

●   ●   ●

went walking.

○   ●   ●

Soon
he saw some people.

In a village there was much fighting,
much arguing
and calling of names.
You see,
there was a young man who wanted a wife.
But he couldn't find a good one.
He disliked all the women he saw.
Also,
he was quite conceited.

THIS,
this interested Wichikapache.
So he turned into a woman.

He turned into a woman.

Now
he was a beautiful woman.
He got a team of wolves
to draw his sled
into the village.
Also,
the wolves then put up his tent.

The young man quickly liked this woman.

"Family,"
the man said,
"please invite her."

Wichikapache
was invited there.

The mother said,
"My son desires to marry you."

"Well
I'll tell you,"
Wichikapache said,
"the very reason I ran from my home
and ended up here
was because so many men wanted
to marry me.
My elder brother got so tired
of men coming around
he finally said, Go Away!"

The old woman said,
"Same with my son.
He went all over
but ended up here
because so many women wanted
to marry him.
He thought he could build a house
and live quietly.
But as you see
it was not true.
It kept going on."

Well,
finally they met.

They were married
a long time.

Wichikapache was a good wife.
But, after a while,
he wanted to move on.
Before he did he had babies.
They happened to be wolf cubs.
He tied them up
and sent a messenger
to the grandparents.
Then,
in the night,
he left.
The grandparents arrived,
took up the babies,
and said, "These are wolf cubs!"

"Oh no!"
the grandfather cried out,
"that wife was Wichikapache!"

The others laughed
at the husband
because of his wolf children.

"It's really a great thing
that he has these wolf babies,"
one man said.
"Now
this great conceited man
hides nothing.
We know he had Wichikapache
for a wife!
Ha!"

"A man
for a wife!
Ha!"
one other man said.

Everyone
had his own way
of putting it.

The husband went away.
He said to himself,
"I don't care how good looking she was
that wife.
WICHIKAPACHE
shamed me."

Now
this man went walking.

•　•　•

He came upon a cabin.

He heard a woman's voice inside.

So, he went in
and saw a very round woman.
He said to her, "Round one,
marry me?" *Marry me, he said in an asking voice.*
They got married.

They travelled together,
a long way
they travelled.

Upon arriving back at the man's home
somehow.
somehow
she was no longer very fat.
No longer this way.

WICHIKAPACHE
was waiting for them.
Of course,
Wichikapache.

Wichikapache said,
"What?
you have this beautiful woman
for a wife now?
This woman who is neither too round
or fat?"
Neither one, he saw.
"What about me,
your first wife?"

The man said,
"All right,
go take care of the wolf babies!
Suckle them.
Teeth them on your feet.
Get going!
Go!"

"No!"
Wichikapache said,
"I leave!"
He said this,
laughing to himself.

He went walking.

169

NOTES TO THE POEMS

O FTEN *after a single performance or exchange of stories in Cree communities, talk ensues about the tellings. Everyone joins in. Viewpoints of performers and listeners hold equal weight; they could be called "discussions of craft." It is a good time to gain insight, from a Cree point of view, on the role of a teller. Such things as the quantity of tales remembered, the individual talents in presenting repertoires of gestures and voices, the ability to teach an apprentice tales, the knowledge of previous telling "sessions" (which themselves become told about)—all are commonly spoken of as criteria that determine the teller's efficacy.*

One can also approach the teller's role by examining the specifics of an apprenticeship, as well as the seasonal and ceremonial circumstances in which certain stories are told. I've often posed the question to Cree people directly: "What makes a good teller?" Answers were incredibly varied, and in every instance, I received an explicative story in return. They took on the role in order to explain it. For example, this answer from William Smith Smith:

> *The best story teller is one who lets you live if the weather is bad and you are hungry. I'll talk about this more. One man I knew long ago. He told me stories. He watched animals. He heard about animals and talked about them. Out of the talk came something. Once he sat down with me and said: "This story has something about ice fishing in it. You should know this thing. Maybe it won't be easy to hear, inside the story, but it's there. Too easy to find you might think it was too easy to do." Well, then he told me the story. Sure enough, there was*

172

an important thing in it about ice fishing. I heard it and remembered it. Later, I asked myself: What if a wind blew all the other people away and I was alone? Could I catch fish under the ice just going by what I learned in that story? And a little of what I saw done during ice fishing season? I said to myself: Yes! Then I knew he told a good story. Also, it made me laugh.

A.L. Kroeber has written: "Intelligible description of course is not random itemization but an organized presentation with sufficient elucidation of background and context to make it meaningful in the culture to which it is presented. If a body of information conveyed has significance in the originating culture, it will have some significance in the receiving culture, though not an identical one." The Cree talk about where their narratives come from. They discuss how geography, weather, and personality affect narratives and telling styles. They discuss which of their friends "talk interesting," i.e., give them ideas for stories. They even discuss the success and usefulness of variants of even the oldest motifs. I have heard twenty-minute introductions—full of time, place, related and tangential anecdotes—preceding a five-minute story. This talk is natural and useful...

The notes to the translations in this book attempt to illuminate some of the ways the Swampy Cree approach the world, as suggested both by things in the narratives themselves and by related conversations.

I try to make wishes right: Nibènegenesábe considered this the "first" of the narratives, telling it first in any sequence. And the line "but sometimes it doesn't work" invites the impression that the speaker of the narratives is just beginning to try out this new-found wishing talent.

When the squirrels ask the moles "How do we get down there to get home?" we observe an example of interspecies communication found often in Cree narratives. Sometimes specific zoological facts are explicated. One example occurs in a story having partly to do with the migration of geese. An old goose, one who has flown many migrations, brings a fledgling goose to a hummingbird working in a flower field. The old goose asks the hummingbird: "Please, tell this young one how it is." The hummingbird tells the young goose: "This is your first wandering south. When you are most tired, think of me *who beats my wings many migrations-worth each day*, even when I am not heading south. Think of me, yes, then go on flying to where you can finally dip your wings in water and rest."

This is for turtles, that's why: Bubbles, used here as vehicles for the turtle's laughter, suggest the idea of consciously sending something out from the body, something animals do in many Cree stories. Furthermore, any part of the body, or any of the senses, can develop independent actions. Phrases such as the following are heard: "I sent my ears out to hear rain, while I stayed inside"; "The wolves sent their ears out, and their ears brought back the (snapped) ankle of a moose. So the wolves left for the moose"; "My nose went into four cooking fires." In this Wishing Bone narrative it is also said: "Yesterday I was with my toes in the river." Special focus is put on those parts of the body that have particular relevance to the narrative. (See also the naming-origin "Whose Weaving Melted.")

One time I wished myself / into a moose deer: This narrative was Nibènegenesábe's explanation for the naming of a nearby lake, Loon Lake. The phrase "some of the tears left / to look for sad faces / to fall down" is an example of the Cree's vast vocabulary of animation.

One time I saw / a tree with no animals in it: In another story, the wind is again befriended, this time by a hare who asks it to bring in snow to cover the hare's tracks, thus making it difficult for Fox to find him.

A snake lost his eyes once: Other instances of "camouflage" are occasionally heard in stories. In one, a wolf "plays" a mound of snow by covering himself with snow. This results in his surprising a deer.

Sure I saw the water monster! The line "I couldn't think straight so thought crooked" reveals an interesting relationship between *thought* and consequence, i.e., "which is how I got to be / a snake / come winding out."

In another Cree story, a bear who is hungrily daydreaming and babbling about food suddenly finds himself fat and in a hibernation cave.

There was a man who was very tired: The image of a huge valley as a hammock is related to the process of naming geographical places. Examples are numerous, and it would be useful to have a physiographic map of the area based entirely on Algonquian place names. Some place names are based on land forms found there, others on events which occurred there, and so on. One example, in a metaphorical vein, is a place in North Manitoba named *Achewita hotoowuk* ("Their horns are locked"). This name refers to an area where there are about ten trees whose branches are intertwined, out of separate trunks, high in the air.

Crows are often seen following wolves, partly because they are carrion eaters. But they commonly "tease" wolves, too.

There were two caribou deer: Compare the use of the term "moose deer" in one of the other narratives in this cycle ("One time I wished myself.") Both indicate a form of Cree animal classification. Relationships among animals—how animals are classified, and how flexible those classifications are—is an intricate topic in itself. In one story, for instance, when otters speak underwater to fish they are called "Otter fish"; once back on land, they are called "Otters." Animal classifications extend into areas having to do with totem ancestries. One seldom—except in speaking in a classificatory manner—says the word "Bear" (*Mu skwa*) itself. Instead, the bear is referred to as "old man," or variants thereof.

These narratives were heard and translated between 1967 and 1973, primarily in the area of the Belanger and Cobham rivers.

Tree Old Woman: In this narrative, a girl begins to resemble, in her wrinkling face, whatever she gets close to: a tree, a frog, etc. Mimicry of, or close proximity to, animals can result in a sort of transformation. Another example is found in the naming-origin "Woke into a Heron," in which a girl, after watching and standing near herons, later takes on their characteristics. And in one Wishing Bone narrative ("One day I wished myself"), a man living half his life among frogs begins to resemble one. Again, the actions and physical characteristics of animals are often assimilated into songs and narratives.

Sat in the Center: "Snow snakes," mentioned in this narrative, are those whirls of snow and wind that rush along the surface of the earth.

Rain Straight Down: The phrase "kinds of rain" indicates a kind of metaphor in this narrative. I have seen Cree point to herons dripping water as they rise, and in fact speaking of it in a classificatory sense, as "heron rain."

Whose Weaving Melted: In many narratives, the parts of the body most relevant to the story are singled out, as in this one which contains the phrase "waited for her toes and face," as well as "everyone took his nose and mouth / inside."

Born Tying Knots: This is the only name in this selection given *at* birth. The line "The fire got loose its own way" implies a cognitive action by the fire. In another Cree story, a fire, out on its own, sits on wet leaves. "I can't live here!" it says; "Let me think about this. Over there is a dry place for me to live."

Walked toward the Lynx: The term *Pisewatik* is occasionally used to mean "Wild cat tree," a tree whose roots are used for the cure of cramps and muscle spasms, and/or a tree with the mentioned "scratch marks" of a lynx on it.

Many Talks: In this narrative the girl "grinned all through / the telling." In other words, she took on the "grinning" characteristic of

176

the catfish about which she spoke. Such animal mimicry would naturally be considered a good dramatic practice, since vocal and facial imitations are effective devices in story performances.

Many Voices: Again in this narrative one can see a definite connection between *thinking* and subsequent events: ". . . Maybe she was *thinking* / of a fox barking, long ago, / and that thinking CAME OUT LOUD."

Always Surprised: "In these stories, animals can be (directly) involved in names," Makidemewabe said. That is, animals can be aware of the process of earning a name, as indicated in the first line of this narrative: "Owls started this."

It is interesting to compare the closing lines of the naming-origin "Followed the Heron Shade": "Finally, we saw how those herons / were giving us her name."

Saw through to the Bottom: Note the lines "because we knew a mud fish / spoke out mud / into the water, OUT OF HIS MOUTH, / so he would always have a muddy place to swim." I have heard only one other Cree narrative in which an animal physiologically created his own environment. In that story, a fish got inside a bubble it blew from its "mouth spit" and travelled through rapids, protected from, and bouncing off, sharp rocks.

NOTES TO THE SHORT POEMS

That far north beast: This poem was told by Joseph Big Sandy, who said he was speaking in it of a Windigo. (See notes to the tale.)

With you I want to carve: Told by Joseph Big Sandy. "Bird sticks" are rattle-sticks used to accompany songs in which curing medicines are requested from certain birds. If the stick works, it may become the bird itself.

You don't believe it? Told by Joseph Big Sandy, who said it came out of an argument. According to him, several men were sitting on a porch when another man came up to them, saying: "I had a rough journey. On my way here I fell over some rocks. Later I fell over some shadow-roots" (i.e., the shadows *of* thick, surfaced tree roots). An argument ensued among the men as to whether shadows actually have "thickness." Joseph stated: "Later this poem came from me."

Skeleton of a bear: Told by John Rains, who commented: "Many nights I slept under a bear quilt, and thought of the bear. The poem came from that."

Owl; The goose is frozen in the lake; and *Old jay, loudmouth of the tree!* These three poems were told by Isaac Greys during a very long session of *tellings* near Otter Lake in Manitoba (August, 1967).

Now we are outside: Told by Yakwama Yetum, who said: "This is an old story, told by my grandfather. I tell it each spring."

In my illness . . . : Told by Charles Hoyt Backward Owl, who said it recounts what occurred during an illness accompanied by a high fever.

A small lynx: Told by Small Lynx, a man living (in 1970) near Cormorant Lake, Manitoba. He said he lost his parents at a young age.

The poems *I wake and see my wife; I'm in trouble swimming; If I had such cleverness; The trees are creaking; I am the poorest one;* and *That man!* were all told by John Rains.

The two poems *I wanted to travel with the porcupine* and *I never saw the Wolverine* were told by Joseph Badfoot Michael.

178

1. The discussion of names between Wīchikäpäćhe and the young ptarmigan he encounters deserves comment. Note that, initially, the ptarmigan give several false names. Among many Cree, it is considered improper to ask someone's name directly. A third party may introduce you. Often, if one does ask a name directly, he receives a "joking" answer, if any. In addition, the description of the other ptarmigan flying up and startling Wīchikäpäćhe, thus validating the name "small winged startlers," illustrates one way in which animals were named.

2. Note the description of an old Cree dance, the "goose dance," in which much goose behavior is mimicked.

3. In other Cree stories I have heard, talk with skunks is often somewhat more "delicate" and humorous than that with most other animals. One can see that Wīchikäpäćht, even in his trickery, is a bit patronizing to the skunks, too.

4. The Windigo (there are varied pronunciations of this name throughout the Algonquian world) is a powerful, man-eating giant whose appetite is voracious and seemingly insatiable. There are both male and female Windigos. One of its many frightening attributes is that it is widely considered to have an ice heart. Windigos are completely impervious to cold and wear no clothes, although they occasionally cover themselves with spruce gum. Some say Windigos are most active in winter, others say in months when no snow is on the ground, because then their presence is not given away by tracks. Theories of origin are numerous. Some believe Windigos are misguided, transformed humans born in historical time out of the invention of incredibly cruel, devious shamans. Other Cree assert that Windigos have always lived on earth. Still others believe Windigos represent all those who have died of starvation.

Windigos are complex figures. The relationship between belief and behavior in relation to Windigos is discussed at great length by M.I. Reicher in his paper "Windigo Psychosis" (Proceedings of the Spring, 1960, Meeting of the American Ethnological Society). This paper also provides a useful geographic list of Windigo-derived place names.

179

5. After Wīchikäpāćhe's transformation into a woman, Nibènegenesábe keeps the male gender active in speaking of him: "He turned into a woman. / Now / *he* was a beautiful woman. / *He* got a team of wolves / to draw his sled."

I inquired about this. Nibènegenesábe explained: "If Wīchikäpāćhe turned a (male) animal into a woman animal *forever*, then it would be called 'she.' But Wīchikäpāćhe stayed a man (even though) he was a wife and gave birth. It was part of the trick, the scheme. And he knew things would end up the way they did. He knew he would turn back into Wīchikäpāćhe again."

6. Nibènegenesábe was a Swampy Cree. He mentioned that he had travelled west at various times. L. Bloomfield in his monographs "Sacred Stories of the Sweet Grass Cree" (National Museum of Canada, Bulletin No. 60) and "Plains Cree Texts" (American Ethnological Society, Vol. XVI) has gathered two tales using motifs comparable to those in this tale. The latter monograph contains a Plains Cree tale of great similarity. Nibènegenesábe once said: "Wīchikäpāćhe travelled, the stories travelled with him."